Stay Close
To
The Good Shepherd
God Bless
Pastor Jim
IS. 40:31

Thanks for Helping My Man
Love & Blessings
May

Endorsements

AS I READ THE SHORT devotional chapters in *A Shepherd's Heart*, I thought of Jesus, when He said, "Feed my sheep." These stories inspired, encouraged, challenged, and blessed me; this sheep was fed. Pastor Jim, you are clearly a shepherd with a big and caring heart. Thank you for faithfully obeying the Great Shepherd by continuing to feed the sheep: both those that follow, and those that tend to wander away. Thank you for feeding me!

—Gigi Graham
  Daughter of Reverend Billy Graham

A SHEPHERD'S HEART: REAL PEOPLE, real situations, real victories. What an encouraging read. Like taking fresh vitamins for the soul. I love these inspiring stories about everyday folks who overcome struggles through the love and guidance of Jesus and His people.

—Jack "Murf the Surf" Murphy
  CEO, Sonshine Adventures, Inc.

THE SCRIPTURE OFTEN USES THE term *Shepherd* as a metaphor to describe our Lord Jesus. A thorough study of the history of shepherds throughout the Middle East offers a perfect illustration of the preeminence of the Chief Shepherd who lovingly cares for His sheep. Likewise, the importance of the Under Shepherd, as outlined in 1 Peter 5, is one who carries out the will of the Chief Shepherd.

Pastor Jim Brissey, along with his devoted wife, Jean, has faithfully demonstrated the valued qualities and unfathomable influence of the office of the Under Shepherd. Their leadership, now approaching 1000 ministry outreaches from Higher Ground Ministries in Central Florida, stands as an authentic testimony to their resolute quest to follow in the Lord's footsteps.

I count it a distinct privilege to recommend to you *A Shepherd's Heart*. As you peruse this sweet devotional, you just can't help but sense the heartbeat of the Good Shepherd.

—Bob D'Andrea

Founder and President,
Christian Television Network

More Endorsements

FROM THE CELLBLOCKS OF AMERICA'S prisons to the poverty of Honduras, Pastor Jim Brissey has poured out his mind and heart to lost people. This wonderful book, *A Shepherd's Heart*, is filled with exciting testimonies and miracles of God. Walk with Jim and meet many exciting Biblical personalities. Read, learn, and enjoy the ride!
   —Bill Glass
   Founder, Champions for Life Ministries

MY WIFE AND I ARE truly blessed starting each day with a Spirit-filled message from *A Shepherd's Heart*. This collection of life lessons is anointed by the Holy Spirit, and it reflects the ministry to which Pastors Jim & Jean have been called. Our lives have been truly blessed and enriched over the last ten years by knowing Jim and Jean. Jim's personal transparency and real-life approach to sharing the Gospel provides the authenticity to allow him to spread the word to anyone who is willing to listen. With her exuberance and unbridled passion, Jean exemplifies someone who is filled by the Spirit. They have both made an indelible mark on our lives.

A Shepherd's Heart is a must-read for those who wish to experientially apply God's word to daily living and to enjoy His riches and glories in the fullness of life.
   —William T. Morgan, M.D.
   Bible Teacher & Internist

JIM AND JEAN BRISSEY HAVE regularly volunteered at Putnam Correctional Institution in East Palatka, Florida, for over fourteen years. With a prophet's cry in his voice and as a highly gifted evangelist, Pastor Brissey has faithfully preached the Gospel of the glorious grace of God. Higher Ground Ministries has been one of the most popular program events at this prison and has been used by the Lord to cause many inmates to turn to faith in Christ as an answer to their incarceration problems. Anyone dedicated to ministry will find Jim's words encouraging, thoughtful, and challenging.

The LORD can truly lift us all up to Higher Ground through reading this book.

—DAVID K. MILLER
Senior Chaplain, Putnam Prison

AN EXCELLENT BOOK. A TRULY heart-touching story that will stretch you to new possibilities in places you were not looking to go. When you find yourself boxed in by unendurable circumstances, you will remember how those who must live in the small box of a jail cell can still find their joy. Be prepared to have your compassion expanded to new borders after you read this book.

—DR. KEVIN MCNULTY
Global evangelist;
Co-founder of Christian AdventuresInternational

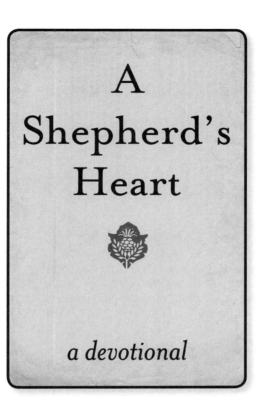

A Shepherd's Heart

a devotional

Jim Brissey

Ambassador International
Greenville, South Carolina & Belfast, Northern Ireland

www.ambassador-international.com

A Shepherd's Heart
A Devotional

© 2014 by Jim Brissey

All rights reserved

Printed in the United States of America

ISBN: 978-1-62020-255-5
eISBN: 978-1-62020-355-2

Unless otherwise indicated, THE HOLY BIBLE, NEW INTERNATIONAL VERSION®, NIV® Copyright © 1973, 1978, 1984, 2011 by Biblica, Inc.™ Used by permission. All rights reserved worldwide.

Scripture taken from the New King James Version®. Copyright © 1982 by Thomas Nelson, Inc. Used by permission. All rights reserved.

Cover design and typesetting: Matthew Mulder
E-book conversion: Anna Riebe

AMBASSADOR INTERNATIONAL
Emerald House
427 Wade Hampton Blvd.
Greenville, SC 29609, USA
www.ambassador-international.com

AMBASSADOR BOOKS
The Mount
2 Woodstock Link
Belfast, BT6 8DD, Northern Ireland, UK
www.ambassadormedia.co.uk

The colophon is a trademark of Ambassador

A Shepherd's Heart is dedicated to Jean, my beautiful bride of thirty-seven years; To our two awesome children, Connie & Jimmy and their godly spouses Steven & Melissa, who all serve tirelessly with us in the ministry; To our amazing grandkids: Megan, Elicia, Gina, Jimmy, David & Joey; And to my sisters, Tica & Roxie, who with their husbands, Larry & Junior, have always been in our corner encouraging and supporting our work in the ministry.

Most of all, *A Shepherd's Heart* is dedicated to the **Great Shepherd, Jesus**—who loves us all more than life.

Table of Contents

Introduction	13
Let Your Light Shine	15
Mary's Marvel	19
For God So Loved the World	23
The Family of God	27
God's Rainbow	29
Business is Business	33
Beautiful Watches	35
A Funny Thing Happened, There on Death Row	37
Love Rolled Away the Stone	45
We Walk Where Jesus Walked	49
Fruit of the Spirit	51
Freedom	55
The Cross	61
A Reckless Reverence	65
Never Quit	67
I Love You More	69
Praises Be!	71
Living Stones	73

Shine	75
Chariots of Fire	79
A Living Letter	81
A Valiant Soldier—with Leprosy	85
Be Strong and of Good Courage	89
Twelve Bells to Glory	93
He has Made All Things Beautiful	95
It's Time for Church	101
Stripes	103
A Tither's Confidence	105
The Man from Galilee	107
They're Beautiful	111
How God Feels About the Lost	115

Introduction

MY SIXTEEN YEARS WORKING WITH PBS were splendid. Rubbing elbows with the likes of Mister Rogers, Captain Kangaroo, and Cookie Monster was a joy. With a six-figure income and an ever-improving golf swing, one could say I was blessed.

Yet, the call of the Spirit to leave the cushy life of corporate climbers and launch out into full-time ministry only grew louder with each passing year.

His calling culminated quite unexpectedly one day. Sitting there at a traffic light, enjoying my air-conditioned new car and my quadraphonic stereo system blasting praise music, I saw a homeless man rummaging through a dumpster. It was raining and unusually cold for Florida.

"Lord, do you want me to get out and help that man?"

"Yes" is all I heard. But in His "yes," the Lord was instructing me not only to get out of that car and help that man, but to get out of my cushy lifestyle and help many others like him.

After praying with my wife, Jean, I resigned from my job the next morning. It was the best decision of my life.

Almost two-score years have come and gone since we stepped out of the boat of our corporate comforts and began walking on the waters of full-time ministry with Jesus.

Sure, we have gotten wet countless times since the day we heard His "Yes." But we would rather be wet water-walkers than dry boat-sitters any day!

Now we rub elbows with the down-and-outers and watch God transform them into up-and-comers . . . one soul at a time.

"Yes!" One could say we are truly blessed!

We pray that this collection of meditations, poems, and a few of our favorite jokes will, in some small way, share with you some of the laughter (and a few of the tears) we have experienced in our journey, since that fateful day we heard and obeyed His "Yes."

Let Your Light Shine

Matthew 5:16

MANNY VALLE WAS A RAMBUNCTIOUS 27-year-old kid who made one very bad decision: a decision that cost him his life. During a routine traffic stop in Coral Gables, Florida over thirty years ago, Manny panicked and shot a police officer. Officer Pena died. Manny spent the next thirty-three years in a six-by-nine-foot cell on Death Row in Starke, Florida. He was allowed out of his cell for one hour, two times per week.

Four years ago, as we were sharing the Gospel from cell to cell on Death Row, God blessed me and my friend "Gator" with the amazing honor of leading Manny to Christ. It was the "real deal."

When we first met Manny, we talked about anything *except* Jesus. We talked about Philly steak sandwiches, the Philadelphia Phillies, the N.Y. Jets, Mustang automobiles, and more. At that time, Manny had been on Death Row for twenty-nine years, and he didn't know Jesus from a can of paint.

God's love was present in a strong way, even as we simply talked about this and that. It was like watching a snowball melt in a microwave as Manny began to realize we weren't there to beat him up with a Bible. It must have been thirty or forty minutes into our conversation before Gator and I began to share our testimonies and explain the difference between "religion" and a relationship with Jesus.

Before we knew it, Manny had one hand raised through the bars holding my hand and the other holding Gator's. Tears ran down his face as we led him in the sinner's prayer, and Manny Valle gave his heart to Jesus. The very first question I asked Manny after he said "Amen," was, "Manny, do you have a Bible?" He said no. At that very second, a volunteer opened the door about sixty feet away and yelled down the Row, "Anybody need a Bible?" The three of us laughed and cried at the same time! "Yes! Right here!" Gator and I signed Manny's Bible, said so long, and went on our way.

Manny became a close friend with Jesus that day. And he soon became a dear friend of mine. Over the past four years, I can't begin to explain how much his letters have meant to me. I drove up to Starke every few months to surprise Manny with a visit: but I was always the one who left Death Row renewed and revived! What a difference Jesus makes! With every letter and every visit, I marveled at Manny's humble and grateful heart. Like a bright light in a dark place, Manny's faith and sense of humor changed the atmosphere. He was a Christian. He was a friend.

God blessed me with a wonderful three hour visit with Manny, while he was on death watch, just a few days before he was executed. We laughed more than anything else. Manny was beautifully clothed in the peace that passes all human understanding. Before I said goodbye, he looked me in the eye and said, "Jim, I will meet you at the Pearly Gates with a Philly steak sandwich and a box of cannolis! . . . And give my love to Jean."

Manny was executed at Florida State Prison on Sept. 28, 2011 at 7:04 p.m. They offered him a tranquilizer before escorting him to the death chamber. He refused. Manny died in peace. He died in Christ. We prayed and cried with his family in Starke during his execution. I miss him. Yet, whenever I am feeling blue, I think of Manny's big smile, and my world is a bit brighter.

A candle burned
On the cold, dark row
A graceful fire
A warm Christ-glow

A bit colder now
A bit darker still
The cold dark row
The cold dark row

Mary's Marvel

Mary treasured up these things in her heart.

LUKE 2:19

How Mary must have marveled
That very first Christmas Eve:
Not by power nor by might,
But by His Spirit—just believe!

Shrouded by the quiet
Amidst the hay and straw,
Joseph and the shepherds
Bow down in reverent awe.

The Lord of all creation,
Who made the Sabbath rest,
Decided to Himself come down
And lie at Mary's breast.

The glory-filled small manger
Must have caused the stars to dim;
The promise of the ages,
Now all fulfilled in Him.

In joyful, holy splendor
They journeyed from afar:
Three kings, three gifts, three Persons
One bright and Morning Star.

Gold they brought for kingship:
He is the King of Kings,
The Alpha, the Omega,
Of whom all creation sings.

Incense they brought for priesthood:
Our intercessor, our high priest;
To become the very greatest,
One must first become the least.

Myrrh was brought for burial:
Our blameless sacrifice.
This is chiefly why He came
Nothing less would suffice.

Not by His birth He saved us
Nor to live on Earth He came,
But to give His life a ransom,
Lost sinners to reclaim.

At the foot of an ugly cross
Stared a mother at her son,
As she questioned why she heard
"It is finished, it is done!"

How Mary must have marveled
That very first Easter morn:
"Why seek the living among the dead?
Woman, this is why I was born."

I came to give life to my bride
For I am that I am the Bridegroom;
So hearts would be full like the manger
Not cold like the empty tomb!

For God So Loved the World

> John 3:16

IT'S NOT OFTEN I'M UP before the morning paper arrives, but this is no ordinary day. He's so young, only seventeen, and now a member of the United States Army. They said they'd come for him at 5:00 a.m . . . and that they did. Not 4:59, not 5:01, but 5:00 a.m. sharp. It was the appointed time. We knew it was coming. We know in our hearts it is for the good, but that doesn't make it easy.

The house is painfully quiet right now. My son Jimmy is gone. He left just moments ago, to go to a place called Fort Sill, Oklahoma, to begin basic combat training. Oh, how I will miss him. How I will miss the sound of his laugh, the flash of his smile, the smell of his aftershave as he whisks by on his way to a date. No doubt the coming weeks and months will be filled with impromptu reminders of my son, my only son, whom I love so much. My memories will comfort me some. We had such good times on the golf course together. Wow, how that guy can hit a golf ball. And he was such a popular kid. I've never seen anyone with more friends than Jimmy. No wonder he made homecoming court two years in a row. Voted the vice-president of the senior class and best looking in the school: imagine that, my son, the best looking! He always did take after his mom.

When Jimmy was a boy he loved baseball. He was an excellent catcher and a darned good shortstop. I'll never forget the big catch he made one year during the important playoff game to save his team from defeat, or the time just a couple of years ago when he stole not only second and then third base, but stole home plate also. He led his team in stolen bases. He was so quick, so agile, so full of life and promise. Where did all the years go?

God help him now to be strong. Comfort him when he feels so alone. Guard his heart as the drill sergeant makes sport of him. How it pricks my heart to think of that. He's on his own now. Daddy can't take his place this time. He must do it on his own. Help him not to quit when his body tells him to and to find hope when it eludes those around him. Help him, oh God, to know that he is not alone, for our prayers and our hearts are with him. Give your angels charge over him and protect him from the evil one and from himself.

As Christians we love to celebrate Christmas. Joy to the world! A Savior has come to demonstrate God's great love and save us from our sins. "For God so loved the world that He gave His only son." Every year around Christmas time, it seems the whole world is touched by a special grace. Many times we see the effects of Christmas in the faces of those we encounter in the mall or across the dinner table. There is a glow that seems to overshadow the struggles of life. There is a richness of peace that seems to permeate the air. "For unto us a child is born . . . unto us a son is given."

John the beloved tells us in his gospel, "In the beginning was the word and the word was with God and the word was God. The word became flesh and dwelt among us." This morning, in the shadow of my son's departure, I more fully appreciate what God has done. Somehow, though in a small way, I have tasted a new part of God's plan and of His Christmas. How quiet heaven must have seemed to the Father as the world received its Christ, as our Lord and elder brother stepped from eternity's heaven to put on an earth-suit. How the Father's heart must have broken on that first Christmas morn. What a void Jesus must have left in heaven when the appointed time came. How strange it must have seemed for heaven to be without

His laughter, and how dark it must have seemed without His smile. Oh, how it must have stabbed the Father's heart, when the soldiers mocked and crucified His son.

"For God so loved . . . he gave his one and only Son . . ." (John 3:16). This indeed is a love beyond mine. It is a love beyond understanding or finding out. "See what great love the Father has lavished on us, that we should be called children of God!" (1 John 3:1a). Oh, Christian, let us not take this love lightly or allow it to be without effect. Great is the sacrifice of our heavenly Father! Mighty is the work of His only son. This life indeed will have its troubles, but we must remember: He has overcome the world!

In the hours ahead my mind will undoubtedly be filled with baseball games and bicycle races, birthday parties and family vacations, Christmases and special times with loved ones. Life is filled with change, and though change may be for the good, it is not always easy.

Lord, be with my son. Keep him safe from harm. Watch over him and protect him from his enemies and himself. Keep him in your care and in your will. Help him—and us—to live in such a way that we are mindful always of your great love. Reassure our fearful hearts that you are love . . . and your love never fails!

The Family of God

How great is the love the Father has lavished on us.

1 John 3:1

I AM A PART OF the family of God. I have been born again! I'm saved by grace, empowered by joy, inspired by love, protected by angels, and established in His word.

There's a song in my heart, a bounce in my step, a light in my eyes, and His name is always on my lips. I'm no longer ashamed, alone, afraid, or abandoned. God is my Father, Jesus my brother, and my guide is none other than the stone-rolling, death-defying, awe-inspiring Spirit of the Living God!

I am a part of the family of God. I have a place set at the Master's table. But before my Father calls me home, to sit at table with all the saints . . .

He has work here for me—that must be done.

There's a race here for me—that must be run.

And battles right here—that must be won.

So, I'll work like there's no tomorrow, dance like nobody's watching, and run with the fire of God. I'm a giver, not a taker; a doer, not a faker. I'll walk the walk and talk the talk, for I am a part of the family of God.

I will not flee, fear, fail, or falter—but with faith I'll fight the fight.

I am a part of the family of God!

I have been born again!

God's Rainbow

I have set my rainbow in the clouds.

GENESIS 9:13

Many colors make the rainbow,
All shining in one accord;
United by His promise
Is the rainbow of the Lord.

They say it takes not only rain
But also bright sunshine
Before we all can clearly see
His ribbon so divine.

Without all its bright colors
The rainbow's incomplete.
Before He went to Calvary,
He washed His good friends' feet.

He took our sin at Calvary,
We know He despised the shame;
But for full joy endured the cross
And said, "I'll rise again!"

Like Joseph's coat of colors—
Once new, but then was torn—
So did the Son of Man become,
As He wore His crown of thorns.

The promise of the Father,
The Son gave all He could,
Angels standing ready
As the spikes went in the wood.

"Father please forgive them,
For they know not what they do!"
If I may be so bold my friend:
Has He forgiven you?

Oh, blessed be the rainbow,
The rainbow of the king;
Colored with joy and victory—
He died to steal death's sting!

He rose again as He said He would,
I'm sure you know the story;
But do you know the mystery
Of Christ in you, the hope of glory?

There's forgiveness in no other,
The price He paid was great,
So seek the man from Galilee
Before it is too late.

To err is human, said the poet,
Forgiveness is divine;
He'll turn your sorrow into joy,
So receive the Son—and shine.

Oh, blessed be God's rainbow,
Made of all those born again.
Oh, blessed be God's rainbow—
His rainbow's made of men!

Business is Business

A merry heart does good like a medicine.

Proverbs 17:22

MISS CONNIE WAS AN EXCELLENT teacher. She was always looking for new and creative ways to motivate her students to pay attention and do their very best. One day she brought a CD player into class, and offered it as a prize to the student who could give the correct answer to a most important question.

"Who was the greatest man who ever lived?" she asked.

Immediately a hand shot up in the back of the room. It belonged to a little Irish boy named Ryan. In a thick Irish brogue, he shouted, "It was Saint Patrick." The teacher responded, "Good answer, Ryan. Saint Patrick was a great man, but he wasn't the greatest."

A young Scottish boy named Sean raised his hand. Miss Connie asked, "What do you think, Sean?" In a thick Scottish accent, he confidently said, "Why, it must have been Saint Andrew." With an encouraging tone,

Miss Connie said, "Good guess, Sean. Saint Andrew was a great man, but I'm sorry, that's not the correct answer."

One more brave student raised his hand. It was a little Jewish boy by the name of Seth. "Miss Connie, I know who the greatest man was," he exclaimed with full assurance. "It was Jesus," he said. "That's correct, Seth; come up a receive your prize!"

As Miss Connie was handing little Seth the CD player, she leaned over and whispered in his ear, "Seth, you gave the right answer, but aren't you Jewish? I'm surprised you would say Jesus was the greatest man who ever lived." Seth didn't miss a beat. "Miss Connie, yes, I am Jewish. And I know the greatest man was really Moses—but business is business!"

Beautiful Watches

My God will provide all of your needs.

Philippians 4:19

CANCHIAS, HONDURAS, CHANGED US. WE arrived on a mission to teach, but departed as students most blessed.

Early one morning our core team was graced with an unforgettable tour of this very poor village, where naked brown children and kind, toothless women greeted us at every turn. We discovered that the small dwellings with dirt floors and cut-out windows were more than huts. They were homes. Although the Canchians had no electricity or running water, they had each other and a remarkable, almost contagious, resilience.

Nancy lived in one of the small huts. She was five years old and had never worn a pair of shoes. Her smile eclipsed her surroundings as we placed new sandals on her feet.

We saw many humbling sights and met many precious souls in Canchias. Each one touched our heart with a warmth only God could give. At the end of our expedition I asked our guide, "Of all the needs you have here in Canchias, what are your greatest needs?"

"Needs? We have no needs," he replied. "The Lord provides all of our needs. You Americans have beautiful watches, but you have no time!"

Later that afternoon, while building a church in a nearby town, my watch band broke. Not having the heart to repair it, I carried that watch in my pocket for the next two years. Whenever I reached into my pocket to check the time, I could see that Honduran man's smiling face, and I could hear his voice saying: "You Americans have beautiful watches, but you have no time!"

A Funny Thing Happened, There on Death Row

I was in prison and you visited me.

MATTHEW 25:36

ACTUALLY, IT WASN'T FUNNY AT all. It was glorious!

In the past twenty years, we have held hundreds of meetings in twelve different prisons in the U.S. and two in Honduras. Yet, I could count on one hand the times we encountered God's grace like we did yesterday at the Death Row hospital in Florida's Raiford maximum security prison.

I've known "Lucky" (Lloyd Duest) for a little more than three of his twenty-seven years on Death Row. He was a strong Christian when we met him, and he has continued to be one for most of his years living on Death Row. His faith shines in that dark place like a candle in the black of night.

God has used this man as a secret source of hope and strength in my walk. The resilience of his lively walk with Jesus, while confined in his six-by-nine-foot cell, has humbled and inspired me more times than I can count. Like the time a couple of years ago when I was so frustrated working with forty-two churches, trying to host a large homeless outreach in Daytona Beach. I received a letter in the mail from Lucky, saying he was with us in spirit—and he included a check for $100.

Or the time last year when I was again ready to throw in the towel. Here came a letter from Lucky telling me that his cancer was back, but he raved about the goodness of God, and how blessed he is to know Him.

Or just a few months ago, when I was bellyaching to God because the funds weren't coming in to cover the cost of our Honduras mission. Here came another letter from Lucky, from the hospital at Death Row, with words of blessing for the Honduras outreach and a check for $200. That was hard enough to take even before I learned that, just two weeks before he wrote the letter, the doctors had to surgically remove his bladder due to the cancer.

What a spoiled, pampered, weak American Christian I am!

Since returning from our last Honduras mission, I had so wanted to go to Raiford and hug Lucky's neck and thank him for being such a source of strength and faith to me. Yet, there seemed to be an extra measure of resistance for me to get there: my father-in-law's cancer; now my sister-in-law's cancer diagnosis; my wife getting hit with painful shingles; the ongoing work of trying (too hard) to get our struggling church "in the black"; keeping up with our outreach schedule; all while planning five new mission trips; etc.

After receiving a call from a dear friend telling me that the doctors are saying that Lucky is not long for this world, I cleared the deck and made the trek to Raiford. I've been in many prisons and on Death Row many times, but never in the Death Row hospital. It was worse than even I imagined.

It was filthy and disgusting. It smelled like a bad nursing home and other than the little sign that said "Hospital" on the front door, there was not one hint of anything medical throughout the building. Paint was falling off the walls like a condemned tenement building, and large boards littered the stairwells. The correctional officers were loud, annoyed with me, and abrasive. One guard joked loudly to another guard, for my benefit, about how he "needed to get saved" as they escorted me down a long, God-awful row of six-by-nine-foot cinderblock rooms sealed with thick metal doors, with only a four-by-eighteen-inch strip of glass connecting them with the outside world.

The two officers unlocked Lucky's door. They are required to stand guard at the open door for the duration of my visit. This seemed to annoy them greatly, to the point that they incessantly chattered with each other at a louder than normal volume, and they had their walkie-talkies turned up full blast. This was apparently all some kind of twisted pay-back: for what, I don't know.

Whatever distraction they were trying to create quickly vanished in the joy of Lucky's surprise to see me. I was humbled by the honor the Lord was anointing me with, to be able to actually hug my close friend for the first time since I had known him. I don't know if I have ever been hugged like that before. All 108 pounds of him hugged me as if he was trying to squeeze the Christ right out of me. Perhaps he was. Perhaps he did.

Even amidst the boisterous noises directed our way from the guards and all the other noise from the hallway, we had an incredible visit. Lucky managed to sit up. He showed me the feeding tube in his stomach and a stamped, addressed letter to me at the end of his bed. Both sights hit me like a brick.

We sat in his hospital room and visited like long-lost school pals. We read scriptures aloud. The noise from the hall was such that I had to read very loud just so he could hear me, even though I was only three feet away from him. He drank in every word of Psalm 91 and Revelation chapter 22. We had a word of prayer together. God was present in a tangible way.

I so wanted to give this dear man something to thank him for the encouragement and inspiration he has been to me. But prison regulations prohibit us from leaving anything with inmates. Anything material, that is. So I said, "Lucky, I want to sing a song in your honor." He said, "Let's sing."

I began to sing "Amazing Grace." Lucky's voice was quiet and weak, so I began to sing just as loud as I could . . . and the most amazing thing happened.

Before I even got to "how sweet the sound," a holy and reverent hush hit that place. And I don't mean only that pitiful, tiny, poor excuse for a hospital room—I mean the entire building. As if on cue, every one of the six correctional officers on that row turned their walkie-talkies off. You could have heard a pin drop. No one was making a sound. It was as if the Holy Spirit put the whole building on lock-down—and without asking anyone's permission. The Presence of God was as thick as a cloud, and I felt the energy of His Spirit as I sang all the louder.

The acoustics of the cinderblock hallway carried the song throughout the building, but there truly was more going on than simply acoustics. The living God had His hand on us.

As I began to sing "I once was lost, but now am found, was blind but now I see," what sounded like the voice of a large black man from probably fifty feet away started to harmonize the song in a way I will never forget. It was holy. It was surreal. It was an unforgettable encounter with the One whose grace truly is amazing.

When we finished singing "praise God, praise God," Lucky just sat there shaking his head, saying over and over again, "unbelievable; unbelievable."

We talked for several more minutes, and Lucky pulled his prayer list from his Bible and pointed to "Higher Ground Ministries" on the very top of his list. There were probably fifty names on his prayer list, including my family, my father-in-law, May, Ginny, Joyce, as well some others who are already dancing on streets of gold. Lucky and I prayed together, and then it was time for me to go.

As I rejoined my two escorts, there was still complete silence in the entire building. Not one sound. This was surreal. It was holy.

The guards led me down the hall, down the trashy, paint-chipped stairs, down the first-floor hallway and there, too . . . absolute silence. Several prisoners sat on a bench near the exit and just stared at the three of us as we walked toward them; they were motionless and silent. Literally, the only sound I heard the entire way out of the hospital was from one of the guards. Right before he opened the door for me to leave the building, he—completely out of character—apologized for the condition of the building, and said they needed to clean it up.

The entire two-hour drive home yesterday, all day yesterday—and even now as I write this—I am clothed in a renewed awareness of how truly amazing God's grace and love really is. That He would save and use a wretch like me.

Thank you, Lucky. Thank you, Lord.

Love Rolled Away the Stone

The angel of the Lord rolled back the stone.
                                    MATTHEW 28:2

Cast your lots for clothes you stripped
My beard is torn, my back is whipped
Put the nails deep in my bone
Love soon will roll away the stone

You are the branches and I the vine
So keep your sponge of gall and wine
I'll take your sin as if my own
Love soon will roll away the stone

Take your spear and split my side
It is for you I'm crucified
My blood your sins all did atone
Love soon will roll away the stone

So take my lifeless body down
Remove my thorny, bloodied crown
And place me in my tomb alone
Love soon will roll away the stone

Let heaven and earth rejoice in me
Love has triumphed through a cursed tree
Sound loud the trumpet, let all be shown
My love has rolled away the stone

I have risen just as I said
The very firstborn from the dead
From this moment on you're not alone
My love has rolled away the stone

Receive your new birth from above
As in the Jordan, a falling dove
Remember truth, a mustard seed sown
My love has rolled away the stone

Troubles and trials in this life are near
Be strong, take heart, be of good cheer
I sought you out, you are my own
My love has rolled away the stone

I will finish what I have begun
You are my workmanship and my son
Not one of you will I disown
My love has rolled away the stone

I have conquered all hell's damnation
I am the one and true foundation
Seated on my rightful throne
Soon love will bring my children home

We Walk Where Jesus Walked

Whoever claims to live in Him must walk as Jesus did.
1 John 2:6

WHILE IN ISRAEL, WE WALKED where Jesus walked. It was surreal. It was holy.

We prayed in Bethlehem and touched the olive trees of Gethsemane. We sang in Cana, climbed the Sermon Mount, and gazed at Calvary. We were awestruck on the shores of Galilee as we heard the Spirit whisper quietly, "Feed my sheep."

Nazareth, Capernaum, Jerusalem, and Golgotha left their mark on our very souls. The Bible will never be the same since we walked where Jesus walked. Yes, we walked where Jesus walked!

Though many miles from Bethlehem now, we are close to Jesus still. Walking with the homeless, the orphan, the prisoner, we walk where Jesus walked.

May we always be covered in the dust of our Rabbi . . . as we walk where Jesus walked! Yes! We walk where Jesus walked!

Fruit of the Spirit

For the fruit of the Spirit is love.

GALATIANS 5:22

Love was wrapped up in a blanket
And placed within a manger;
Though the world was made by Him,
He entered it a stranger.

Joy in the person of Jesus
Came down from heaven above;
He humbly entered the Jordan
And was baptized with a dove.

Peace He is the Prince of,
He sought no earthly crown.
"No one takes my life from me,
For I freely lay it down."

Patience was personified
As He faced the Roman whips;
Pilate's threats and curses
Brought silence from His lips.

Kindness He exemplified
As He hung between two thieves:
Amidst the nails and thorns He pled,
"Father, forgive them, please."

Goodness was wrapped up in a blanket
And placed in a borrowed grave—
Yet rose victorious on the third day;
He died to make death His slave!

Faithfulness He promises
To all who go His way,
So seek ye first His kingdom
On this holy Christmas day.

Gentleness a garment,
Given by the King of Kings;
Wrap it tightly 'round thee
And hear all of heaven sing.

Self-control I've often found
An elusive quality;
The "me, myself, and I" must die—
To be reborn on bended knee.

The manger, cross, and empty tomb—
The inseparable Trinity;
All wrapped inside a simple man:
A man from Galilee.

Freedom

It is for freedom that Christ has set us free.

GALATIANS 5:1

TEARS OF JOY RAN FREELY down the faces of many parents on Thursday. It was graduation time for Charlie Battery. They had completed their basic combat training in the United States Army. Never have I been more proud as a parent. Never have I been as proud to be an American. 205 boys began basic training, 189 men graduated, about a dozen with honors. Our Jimmy was one of the honor grads. Wow! What a thrill to see the soldiers snap to attention and carry out their duties with such precision. Hooooah! Each soldier was in uniform, from their spit-polished shoes to their shiny silver and brass medals. They were all in uniform, all immaculate. I don't think there was a dry eye in the place when the Army band played the "Star-Spangled Banner." Never before had I heard it played with such passion and purpose. The price these young men had paid to earn the right to be called *soldier* was evident. It had not been easy. There was great sacrifice and hard work involved. As we watched each soldier called by name to receive his diploma, one could not escape the obvious greater sacrifice these young men represented. So many soldiers have gone before them, many sacrificing their lives to earn and protect the freedom we Americans so often take for granted. In the recesses of my mind, I heard a whisper, "Give me liberty, or Give me death!"

Amid such displays of freedom and sacrifice, my thoughts centered on our Christian heritage. How many patriots of the faith have gone before us, laying down their lives for the gospel? Yet these saints of God are just a small shadow of the ultimate price that was paid for our freedom long ago on an old wooden cross. "It is for freedom that Christ has set us free" (Galatians 5:1a). Oh, Christian, may we never take this freedom for granted, or ignore such a great salvation. "So if the Son sets you free, you will be free indeed" (John 8:36). Let freedom ring in the hearts of God's people as we celebrate victory over sin, death, hell, and the grave. May we always press on to the mark with passion and purpose. May we never drop out or settle for mediocrity, but live in such a way as to joyfully anticipate the words our Savior reserves for those who graduate with honors: "Well done, good and faithful servant!" (Matthew 25:23a).

The soldiers of Charlie Battery moved with such unity. They moved as one. They obviously understood teamwork and working together to accomplish a common goal.

How the kingdom of God would advance if we Christians could put away petty differences and move as one. One of the things we found so interesting about military life is that every soldier has a battle buddy. This is someone you are trained closely with to carry out the duties of the day, be it in the mess hall or a foxhole: someone you are accountable to and on whom you can depend for even your very life. How we Christians each need a battle buddy. Maybe that's why Jesus sent out the disciples two by two. Perhaps even then Jesus knew that He was going to need help carrying His cross, and He knew we would need help carrying ours. Though He was the Son of God, Christ fell under the weight of His cross. We too stumble and fall. Lord, send us battle buddies to help us in the fight of faith and save us from the pride that wants to go it alone.

Each soldier in Charlie Battery obviously took great pride in the uniform they wore. They knew what it stood for. They knew where it had brought them from, and they had a sober sense of where it may lead. As the troops were in formation, the drill sergeants walked up and down the ranks with an eye for detail, making sure that every soldier was in uniform. Ephesians 6:11, 17 tells us (my paraphrase, based on the Amplified Version): "Put on God's whole armor [the armor of a heavy-armed soldier] to stand against the devil. . . . Stand therefore with the belt of truth, the breastplate of integrity, with your feet shod in preparation to face the enemy with the gospel of peace, with the shield of faith, the helmet of salvation, and the sword of the Spirit, which is the word of God."

Lord, send your Holy Spirit as a heavenly drill instructor, making sure we won't go into battle ill-prepared. Help us to rejoice in full uniform, mindful of where you have brought us from and sober-minded about where you may lead us.

As we enjoyed a good meal with our son, we must have asked a million questions about his new life as a soldier. He had grown so in the past ten weeks. Jean asked if they got enough water to drink during their long marches. "Affirmative," he said reflexively. "It's not optional. We drink when given the command: "D-r-i-n-k . . . w-a-t-e-r!" It seems the commanding officers have learned from experience that a dehydrated soldier is ineffective. When dehydrated, they run the risk of falling out of step, or worse yet, passing out. For the soldier in a hundred-mile march, drinking water is not a luxury: it is a necessity. One of our final marching orders in the Bible is found in the last chapter, Revelation 22:17, "The Holy Spirit and the Bride say, 'Come, . . . D-r-i-n-k . . . w-a-t-e-r." The water that John the beloved is writing about is the same water Jesus spoke of with the woman at the well. It is living water, given to sustain us. It's not optional! Oh, God, give us ears to hear your life giving command: "D-r-i-n-k . . . w-a-t-e-r!!!" Help us to drink so we won't become ineffective, or fall out of step with your Spirit. Teach us to be filled and on the lookout for one who may be thirsty or fallen from the march.

Our son is still many miles from us. Yet somehow he seems closer since our visit to Fort Sill. The melodic cadence of the soldiers marching still echoes in my mind. My heart remains strangely warmed by the men of Charlie Battery and the flag they salute. Oh, God, keep our good soldier in your care. May your angels camp 'round about him. Keep him in step always with your Spirit, in full uniform for the battle. Above all, dear God, please remind him often to: *"D-r-i-n-k . . . w-a-t-e-r!"*

The Cross

I will boast of nothing except the cross.

GALATIANS 6:14

The cross is stained red
With the blood that was shed
On a tree
On dark Calvary;

The darkness and pain,
Disgrace and the shame,
Made clear for the
World to see:

With a crown of sharp thorns,
Crowds of insults and scorns,
He willingly bled there
For me.

Oh, grave, where is your victory?
Oh, death, where is your sting?
The enemy is defeated!
"King Jesus!" is the song I sing.

Sing loud the cry of victory!
Let all the world behold
The beauty of an empty cross.
And so the story's told

Of a fisher of men from Nazareth
And the Sea of Galilee,
Who caught me in His net of love
And set my spirit free.

His name, above every other,
Should be high and lifted up;
Lift high the name of Jesus
And He'll overflow your cup.

His love and joy and peace
And patience and kindness too,
Are fruit of His Holy Spirit,
Given for me and you.

Seek the fullness of His Spirit
While He can yet be found,
For where the Holy Spirit is
Truth and freedom will abound.

So on Resurrection Sunday
May your hope be raised anew,
In the blessed name of Jesus:
The King of all the Jews.

A Reckless Reverence

David danced with all His might.

II Samuel 6:14

GOD IS CALLING US TO a reckless reverence! In II Samuel 6:14 we see a dancing king: "David danced before the Lord with all his might." I know another King who loves to dance. His name is Jesus and if you are a Christian, He lives on the inside of your heart. So, let Him dance! But remember: He likes to lead! He leads us with His radical reasoning and tells us: "Come now, let us reason together. Though your sins are like scarlet, they shall be white as snow; though they are red as crimson, they shall be like wool" (Isaiah 1:18). All of our sins are forgiven because of His cross. But watch out! As we receive His radical reasoning and move into a reckless reverence, we will see a righteous riot! As He promises in Joel: "I will pour out my Spirit on all people."

The Lord often speaks to me in pictures. One day I was in prayer, and in my mind's eye I saw a restaurant jam-packed with customers. There wasn't an empty seat in the house. The waitress came to the first table and asked, "Can I get you something to drink?" Everyone at the table just looked at her and said, "No, we're not thirsty." The waitress then asked, "Would you like to order something to eat?" The people replied, "No, we're not hungry." This same scenario repeated itself in my mind as the waitress went from table to table, unable to take any drink or food orders. I asked the Lord what He was trying to show me. "This is my church," He said, "it is full of people who are not thirsty or hungry!"

Is anybody thirsty? Are you thirsty enough to get radical with God? When David danced before the Lord with all his might, it caused quite a stir. Even his wife criticized him: "How the king of Israel has distinguished himself today, disrobing in the sight of the slave girls of his servants as any vulgar fellow would." You've got to love David's response to his soon-and-forever-to-be-barren wife, "I will become even more undignified than this . . ." (2 Samuel 6:22a). You go, David! How about you, child of God: will you become more undignified for the Lord? God is calling us to a reckless reverence!

Never Quit

Therefore, since we are surrounded by such a great cloud of witnesses, . . . let us run . . .

HEBREWS 12:1

OUR DAUGHTER CONNIE WAS A true cross-country champion. With her ponytail keeping rhythm like a metronome, Connie ran like the autumn wind. Ranked number four in Hillsborough County, Florida, our *cum laude* grad of the University of South Florida always gave her all. She was poetry in motion.

"Go, Connie, go!" I would yell from the crowd, as she ran with all her heart to the finish line. I cherish the many special memories we share of races so well run.

Amid the stockpile of trophies and medals hides a seventh-place ribbon, her reward for her greatest race. She was in third place with a half mile to go when she sprained her ankle badly, due to a slight misstep. She kept running, but now with a limp. Soon she was in fourth place and then dropped to fifth place. "Go, Connie, go!"

With just a quarter mile to go she fell into sixth place. Grimacing in pain as she crossed the finish line in seventh place, her ankle was swollen larger than a softball. We immediately rushed our faltering track star to the hospital. Thank God it was just a bad sprain.

While waiting to be discharged from the emergency room, Coach Goff arrived with her seventh place ribbon. "Connie, that was the best race you ever ran. You didn't give up. You didn't quit!" Yes! It was her best race indeed. She didn't give up. She didn't quit.

Life is full of hidden missteps, and good people stumble unexpectedly. Divorce, loss of loved ones, financial setbacks and the like can trip even the best of us. Some days we run effortlessly. Some days we run with a limp. But, we run!

God's great cloud of witnesses surrounds us, cheering us to "Press on!" We don't give up. We don't quit. No, we must never give up. *We must never quit!*

I Love You More

Is this the little girl I sang to
As we beheld our mirrored faces?
The one I held and hugged
In her crib with club-feet braces?

The precious one I prayed with
At the tender age of three,
Who gave "Cupcake" milk to drink
And said prayers on bended knees?

Is this the priceless soul who saved
Her dollars when she was ten,
To bless her dad on Father's Day
With the book that has no end?

The Spirit-born evangelist who
Led Sonny & Krissy and friends
To the One who calls the stars by name,
So their new life could begin?

Is this the little drummer girl
Who marched in band and ran?
Our college girl who did us proud
Like the train that said, "I can!"

Is this the girl who took my arm
As I walked her down the aisle,
And gave her hand unto a man
Who promised to make her smile?

The mom who fills her kids each day
With joy and learning too,
Who tucks her boys in bed at night
And whispers, "I love you."

Is this the shepherd we ordained
On that memorable great day,
Our faithful armor bearer
Who walks with us on the way?

The worshipper of Jesus,
Embracing all He has in store.
I know she loves her dad a lot,
But Connie, "I love you more!"

Praises Be!

Grieve not, for the joy of the Lord is your strength.
                                        Nehemiah 8:10

WHILE OFFICER MALONE WAS WORKING late at night one St. Patrick's Day, he noticed a car driving erratically, so he pulled it over. The officer walked up to the driver's window, only to discover that a priest was driving the car. And as much as the officer tried, he could not avoid seeing that the priest had an opened bottle on his lap.

"Have we had a wee bit too much to drink tonight, Father?"

The priest appeared humored by the question. "Not a bit in the world," he retorted.

Officer Malone continued, "Father, with all due respect, I can't help but see that you have an opened bottle there."

"I assure you, my son, it's just me holy water!" the priest exclaimed.

The police officer took the bottle from the priest, drew it to his nose, took a whiff, and then said, "Father, that's not holy water; that's definitely wine."

"Well, praises be," the priest proclaimed, "He did it again!"

Living Stones

You, like living stones, are being built into a spiritual house.
                                                            II Peter 2:5

"I will build my church," the Master cried, "and the gates of hell will not prevail against it."

So where is this church of which He speaks? Is this the church He said He would build or is it that one over there? Neither! His church is not here or there. His church is within us, if we are born of His spirit and washed in His blood.

Peter called it right when he called us "living stones." Peter, "the Rock," knew something about stones. He saw the hungry stones that yearned to become bread after Jesus was tempted in the wilderness. He saw the angry stones in the hands of those so ready to condemn the woman caught in adultery. He saw those same stones become lonely, as those who held them dropped them, turned, and walked away. Peter saw another stone as well—a stone that had been rolled away from the mouth of the tomb of tombs! It was a prophetic stone . . . a stone of purpose . . . a moveable stone, freshly marked with angel's fingerprints.

Oh, Christian, which stone are you? Do you yearn in the wilderness wishing to be something you are not? Do you listen to Satan's lies and temptations as those stones did on the day our Lord was tempted? We were not created to be such stones as those—surely not such as those!

Or are you one of the angry stones? Does accusation and judgment grip you as it did the day our Brother-King wrote with His finger in the dirt? We were not created to be such stones as those; surely not such as those!

Perhaps you are a lonely stone . . . are you one of those? Were you once held tightly but are now all alone? Have your friends and purpose and passion left you? We were not created to be such stones as those . . . surely not such as those!

The church of which our Jesus speaks is not made of such stones as those . . . surely not such as those! He has made us living stones—prophetic stones, stones of purpose, moveable stones fresh with angel prints. He lovingly moves us out of the way—and then He comes forth! Yes, these are the stones we were created to be . . . yes, *surely such stones as these!*

Shine

You will shine like stars.

PHILIPPIANS 2:15

STEPPING OUT OF THE VAN, our mission team of ten beheld a sky like none we had ever seen before. Midnight in rural South Dakota presented a sky resembling black velvet with a thousand shining diamonds scattered about by the hand of God. Magnificent!

The next morning came quickly as our team "pre-prayered" to bring the Good News to the Lakota Indian people on Standing Rock Reservation in Bullhead, S.D. We had learned of the dismal demographics of these hurting people for whom addiction, child abuse, and suicide are the norm. We had also heard that the Indian people were resistant to the white man. Because of this, normally very few salvations are recorded.

Armed with peanut butter and jelly sandwiches and the song of the Lord, we rode into Bullhead with a deep sense of purpose. We were a long way from Daytona Beach, but so very close to the heart of God.

Our hearts burned with God's love as we went house to house with compassion and the power of the Holy Spirit. Many felt the Spirit of the living God and were compelled to receive Him as King. By day three, these precious people were jumping in the boat. The Holy Spirit flowed like a fresh mountain stream as sixty-two Native Americans received Christ in four short days. Wow! As spiritual people, they needed to feel God's presence to know that Jesus is real.

The surnames of these precious people sounded like storybook titles: Redbear; Yellow Earrings; Running Hawk and Elk Nation. Their life stories would break the hardest of hearts. We prayed with many, young and old, men and women, boys and girls. So many of them sad; so many hurting. Many hearts were healed from the ravages of loved ones lost to drugs and suicide. The Balm of Gilead had great impact on Standing Rock Reservation.

We were to hold a celebration at the end of the week with food, music, and the Good News of the gospel outside their sacred PowWow Grounds. The PowWow Grounds are considered holy, and are strictly reserved only for the Lakota Indian celebrations.

Day by day, Jean and her Wings of Praise dance team taught scores of Lakota children a beautiful interpretive dance to the Newsboys' song, "God's Not Dead." At the end of the week, forty-five minutes before our special celebration was to begin, our team was elated: the village elders had invited us to hold our revival meeting right in the middle of their sacred PowWow Grounds.

Our host had warned us repeatedly, "The adult Indian people will not come forward to a white man's altar call." With music and dance, prizes, and preaching the Good News, our team shone like stars in the universe holding out the word of life. Forty-seven more came forward and prayed to receive Jesus during our altar call . . . most were adult Lakota Sioux. Most in tears. All were touched.

Months have come and gone since we walked where these Native Americans walk. However, we now carry their stories, their laughter, and their tears wherever we go.

The Newsboys are right! God's Not Dead, He's Surely Alive, and He's living on the inside of the precious broken Lakota people who now "shine like stars."

Their newborn faith now glistens like diamonds on the black velvet of their broken dreams.

    God's not dead! He's surely alive!

Chariots of Fire

He saw the hills full of horses and chariots of fire.
II Kings 6:17

Chariots of angelic fire
Encamped about the town
Chosen before earth's creation
For a king without a crown.

Shadowed by a painful cross
The humble stable proudly stood
As a lighthouse for the blind,
Birthing hope through a manger of wood.

God so loved, He sent His son
To show us once He was grown
"Let you who be without a sin
Be the first to throw a stone."

The grace-filled Lamb of God,
The embodiment of love;
"I've come to do not my will,
But that of my Father above."

Chariots of angelic fire
Encamped about the town
Chosen before earth's creation
For a king with a thorny crown.

"Abba, Father, please forgive them!"
Cried our Lord, the Prince of Peace.
"This day you'll be in paradise,"
He promised a common thief.

In joyful, heavenly splendor
It was finished, it was done:
The precious babe of Bethlehem
Over sin the battle won.

Rejoice, oh Earth, this Christmas Day:
Not by works, but by His grace.
God has chariots of angelic fire
For all who seek His face!

A Living Letter

Our mouths were filled with laughter.

PSALM 126:2

A DEVOUT CHRISTIAN WOMAN WROTE her sister about an interesting experience she had. She wrote,

"The other day I went up to the local Christian bookstore. While I was there I noticed one of those 'Honk if you love Jesus' bumper stickers. I was feeling particularly sassy that day because I had just come from a thrilling choir performance, followed by a thunderous prayer meeting, so I bought the sticker and put it on my bumper. Boy, am I glad I did. What an uplifting experience that followed. I was stopped at a red light at a busy intersection, just lost in thought about our Lord and how wonderful He is. I didn't even notice that the light had turned green. It is a good thing that someone behind me loves Jesus, because if he hadn't honked, I never would have noticed! I found lots of people who love Jesus! Why, while I was sitting there, the guy behind me started honking like crazy.

Then he leaned out of his window and yelled, 'For the love of God, go! Go! Go! Jesus Christ, go!' What an exuberant cheerleader he was for Jesus! That started everyone honking. I just leaned out of my window and started waving and smiling at all these Jesus-loving people. I even honked my horn a few times to join in the celebration! There must have been a man from Florida back there, because I heard him yelling something about 'sunny beach.' I saw another guy waving at me in a funny way, with only his middle finger stuck up in the air, so I asked my teenage son (in the back seat) what it meant. He said it was probably a Hawaiian good luck sign or something. Well, I've never met anyone from Hawaii before, so I leaned out of my window and gave him the good luck sign back. My son burst out laughing; even he was enjoying this religious experience! A couple of people were so caught up in the joy of the moment that they got out of their cars and started walking over to me. I bet they wanted to pray with me or ask which church I attended, but this is when I noticed that the light had turned green. So I waved to all my brothers and sisters, smiled, and drove through the intersection before the light changed again. I felt kind of sad that I had to leave all my brothers and sisters after they were sharing all that love, so I slowed down the car, leaned out of the window, and gave them all the Hawaiian good luck sign one last time as I drove away.

Praise the Lord for all His wonderful children!"

A Valiant Soldier—
with Leprosy

There is a river that makes glad the city of God.

PSALM 46:4

IN II KINGS CHAPTER 5 we read about an army commander by the name of Naaman. The scriptures tell us that Naaman was "a valiant man, but he had leprosy." He came to Elisha for help, but he didn't like Elisha's prescription to "dip in the Jordan seven times." Naaman was so furious that he left in a huff. No doubt that was so simple it sounded silly—probably like "go jump in a lake" would sound to us today. Naaman angrily said: "Aren't the rivers of Damascus better than these waters of Israel?"

I understand where Naaman was coming from. I was baptized in the Jordan River, and it really is nothing to look at. Naaman almost missed his healing! After some persistence on the part of his servant, though, Naaman agreed and dipped himself in the Jordan. He was made whole again.

Leprosy was such a diabolical disease not because it caused much pain, but because it caused a loss of all sensation in the afflicted areas. The deadened areas made the individual vulnerable to serious injury without even being aware of it. Today I believe America is suffering from an epidemic of leprosy: spiritual leprosy. We have become deadened and hardened to the things of God. We are a great nation, but we have leprosy! Our country is in real danger: not from the Taliban, but from ourselves! Our legislators are taking "under God" out of the Pledge of Allegiance, prayer out of schools, the Ten Commandments out of our courthouses, and our religious leaders are promoting gay marriage and protecting pedophile priests.

What's the answer? I believe the solution is so simple that it sounds silly: we must turn back to God! Christians must emulate Naaman's servant and persist in proclaiming the only real solution: "But seek first his kingdom and his righteousness, and all these things will be given to you as well" (Matthew 6:33). Psalm 46:4 says: "There is a river whose streams make glad the city of God . . ." We must get under the spout where the glory pours out! We must prioritize His presence and spend quality time in worship and

His word. Don't wait for a church service. Get alone with the Lord in your car. Pop in some anointed Christian music and sing out loud to the Lord. Don't worry about what the guy at the red light is going to think! What does that matter? (He probably thinks you're crazy anyway.) By the time you're singing the seventh song on the CD, remember Naaman, and how he found healing as he dipped himself seven times in the river Jordan! Oh, jump! jump! jump in the river!!!

Be Strong and of Good Courage

Joshua 1:6

CHRISTMAS AND CANCER SEEM AUTONOMOUS. The "C" word is not found in any Christmas carols, I know. You never hear anyone singing, "Have yourself a merry little cancer" or "Joy to the world, cancer has come." No, it seems quite strange to hear the two words in the same sentence.

There we were, enjoying the first Christmas with Dad in more than a decade. The welcome we received was even warmer than usual. After all, it was Christmas, and with each Christmas comes a special grace that embraces every relationship. King Jesus' birthdays are always memorable. Families pause from the hustle and bustle of life long enough to talk to each other. There are usually those strolls down memory lane. "Remember when" becomes the common phrase of the day, while loved ones who have passed away seem to walk the earth anew, as vivid memories of Christmases past give new life to those treasured in our hearts.

So, there we were in Dad's Florida room. He was telling us some of those good stories of his army days, as only he can tell them, when the bomb dropped. "The results are in: it's cancer." Those words have since haunted my mind like a bad song you try in vain to forget. He said it with such nonchalance, like "pass the salt" or "more sugar, please." Surely, words announcing cancer should somehow be different, more sinister. Perhaps with some background music. I don't know, they just didn't seem real. Nor did it seem real signing in at the cancer ward at Aventura Hospital on the day after Christmas. Was this a gift from God or a curse from hell, that I should find myself with my dad in such a place at such a time? The answer soon unfolded.

The efficiency of all the health care professionals on this particular hospital ward was impeccable. The staff was cool, calm and courteous—almost too much so. As the nurse searched for a vein in Dad's arm to give him some kind of radium shot, I received a lesson in courage I will not soon forget. He extended his arm cooperatively, laughed, and wished the young man luck. Could this be? We are sitting in a cancer ward, they are testing Dad to see if the cancer has spread . . . and he's laughing. Not a superficial, silly laugh, mind you, but a laugh of faith—a laugh of courage.

The courage and dignity with which my dad is facing this Goliath has done me more good than many sermons. No, being there was no curse. To share such a moment with such a man as this was indeed a gift, a very precious gift. A gift like this cannot be easily given and it can never be taken away.

Dad lay motionless as the gamma ray machine ran through its paces. I sat there watching, my prayers frozen somewhere between faith and disbelief. In that moment, without any fanfare, a pearl from heaven dropped in my heart: "Be strong and of good courage," I heard. Words once spoken by God to Joshua were now helping me clearly see what I was doing in such a place at such a time. No, it was not to be the dutiful son or the cheerful encourager. No, it was to be a student: a student at the feet of a master. God's spirit helped me take notes, not on tablets of paper or stone, but upon my heart. In those precious hours we shared, God magnificently displayed His strength and courage through the living letter of my dad. Never have I witnessed such courage or seen more clearly the peace that only flows from Calvary, as I did on that day.

"I will welcome death with open arms," he said calmly. "I just regret the grief my taking the trip will cause my loved ones." Wow!

Over the years we have experienced many memorable Christmases and received many wonderful gifts. None, however, compares to that Christmas. That Christmas will forever stand apart as special. Some gifts cannot be purchased, but only imparted. Such is the legacy of faith, strength, and courage wrapped by God Himself in an octogenarian named "Dad."

Lord Jesus, be with my dad. Give your angels charge over him. Lead him each day into your tender mercies. Keep him strong in your strength and faith. As you did at the wedding in Cana, please save the best wine for last. Help us, oh God, to be mindful to live one day at a time and to know nothing will come to us this day unless it first passes through your hands in heaven. Happy birthday, Jesus. And thank you!

Twelve Bells to Glory

The peace that passes understanding
The joy of the gospel story
Bringing hope amidst the sound
Of the twelve bells to glory

The trials and temptations
Are now a thing of the past
The body dies, the spirit lives
At home with God at last

The mystery of Easter
The power of the cross of Christ
Eternal words of Jesus
One man, one son, one life

A life so freely given
A ransom fully paid
All our sins forgiven
The atonement has been made

> The angels in heaven are laughing
> At one of Dominick's good stories
> The angels haven't stopped laughing
> Since they heard twelve bells to glory

My brother-in-law, Dominick, was—hands down—the funniest man I ever knew. He made us laugh so hard, with his antics and impressions, that our stomachs hurt from laughing. He was also one of the most troubled souls I've ever known. He was taken prisoner to heroin and subsequently *AIDS*. He made us laugh. Then he made us cry. He broke his parents' heart. They loved him so. We loved him so. God loves him still. On Easter Sunday, 1987, Dominick invited Jesus Christ to be His personal Savior. On Easter Eve, 1994, he was in the last stages of AIDS. His mother told him, "Dom, let go and go be with Jesus." She then went home and prayed to the Lord to take her son on Easter. At exactly the stroke of midnight on Easter Morning, 1994, Dominick went home to be with Jesus.

He has Made All Things Beautiful

There is a time for everything.

ECCLESIASTES 3:1

IT WAS NOT AN UNUSUAL morning. It was Sunday. Perhaps the only thing out of the ordinary was that we were not scurrying to church. Jean and the kids were still sleeping soundly as I moseyed out for the morning paper and turned on the sprinkler to give our thirsty lawn a drink. As I came back in the house, the coffee maker was gurgling loudly, signaling it was ready. A happy sound shrouded in a pleasant aroma.

After a couple of cups of coffee, and reading the sports and business pages, I went back out to adjust the sprinkler and snip a few roses. The Florida sun was rising, playing colorfully through the fine mist so welcomed by the parched soil. Still nothing out of the norm. It was a peaceful, quiet, June morn. Snuggling up on the couch was easy, reaching for my Bible thinking this was a good quiet time. Opening it almost routinely, it fell open to the book of Ecclesiastes. "Ah, yes, the teacher," I thought. My memories took me back to Grandma Jean's funeral, when my wife had read Ecclesiastes chapter three. "There is a time for every season, and a season for every activity under heaven . . ." My eyes ran across the words almost mechanically, and certainly too quickly. Then, as I continued reading, something changed; something was becoming different: ". . . a time to mourn and a time to dance."

The air seemed to become alive, electric, filled with a purposeful presence. "A time to be silent and a time to speak, a time to love and a time to hate, a time for war and a time for peace." By the time I reached verse eleven of this familiar passage, the presence of the Lord in my living room was undeniably special. In my spirit I knew this was a visitation. Without anything out of the ordinary happening around me, I found myself marveling at the wonderful, extraordinary sense of warmth that seemed to rest on me like some heavenly comforter. "He has made everything beautiful in its time. He has also set eternity in the hearts of men; yet they cannot fathom what God has done." As I read this eleventh verse, I knew it would never appear the same to me. It was opening up for me. It seemed to be the reason for which I had opened the Bible. It was becoming for me the message that my heavenly Father was imparting to me. "He has set eternity in the hearts of men, yet they cannot fathom what God has done."

As I closed my eyes in prayer I saw a picture in my mind's eye. My Lord speaks to me so clearly sometimes with pictures. Out of the blue, and in an instant, I saw a little boy. He was quite an ordinary boy, maybe eight or nine years old, with a dirty face and blue jeans.

He had a large bulge in one of his blue jean pockets. "What is this, Lord?" No answer. The youngster reached into his pocket and took out a large, beautiful diamond. It was almost the size of a tennis ball. The boy held the diamond up on the flat palm of his hand. He looked at it intensely, clearly oblivious to its great worth, but strangely mystified by its beauty. In a short moment he put the diamond back in the pocket that seemed to be its home. Immediately, he seemed unaware of its presence. "Lord, what are you trying to show me?' No answer. The picture in my mind expanded. There were other boys, of different sizes, ages, and shapes. They all had bulges in their pockets. "More diamonds, Lord?" More diamonds.

Some of the youngsters didn't seem to care about the diamond in their pocket. Others were fascinated with it. Still others were preoccupied with it, and brought their diamond out into the light quite often, studying and admiring it. They were questioning its purpose and value, totally unaware of its great worth. The Lord reminded me: ""He has made everything beautiful in its time. He has also set eternity in the human heart; yet no one can fathom what God has done from beginning to end" (Ecclesiastes 3:11).

He showed me that we Christians are like boys with diamonds in our pockets. The treasure God has put within each of us is far more precious and valuable than we have the capacity to understand or appreciate. He showed me that, as the little boys grew in stature and wisdom, they would eventually come to a greater awareness of the value of their gems and would ultimately redeem them. So too we grow, and one day we will redeem our treasure.

Paul the apostle tells us in I Corinthians 2:9: "No eye has seen, no ear has heard, no mind has conceived what God has prepared for those who love Him." In II Corinthians 4:7 he reminds us: "We have this treasure in jars of clay to show that this all-surpassing power is from God and not from us."

From Ecclesiastes, the Spirit led me to Psalm 103. Truly He is worthy of our praise, Christian. He has forgiven our sins, healed our diseases, redeemed our life from the pit, and crowned us with His loving kindness. We are the King's kids, crowned with love and compassion. He has given us the gift of faith, worth more than pure gold. As the apostle Peter says, "refined gold resulting in praise, glory and honor."

The strong presence of the Lord seemed to lift as softly and uninvitedly as He had come. There was a holy hush within me. My Lord had come and visited me. He came close to me, closer than my breath. His presence was so real, so tangible. Isn't our God awesome? He takes the ordinary and makes it extraordinary. He takes the routine and fills it with purpose. All our chasing is just that: "a chasing after the wind." But the Spirit, like a wind, blows wherever He pleases, and we cannot tell where He has come from or where He has gone.

Oh, Christian, rejoice! For now we just see through the glass darkly. Yet, in Him, even the darkness sparkles with glimmers of the hope which is to come. Take heart if you find yourself weary and thirsty like the dry ground. He is coming. He is coming to visit and refresh you with His strong grace and strange love. Paul was right, "I consider that our present sufferings are not worth comparing with the glory that will be revealed in us" (Romans 8:18). Yes, all of creation is groaning, waiting for the sons of God to be revealed. Selah!

Maranatha, Lord! Come quickly, Lord Jesus!

It's Time for Church

Forsake not the assembling of yourselves together.
HEBREWS 10:25

IT WAS A COLD SUNDAY morning. The alarm clock sounded and the dutiful wife jumped out of bed. "Come on, Honey. Get up! It's time to get ready for church," she said. The husband didn't budge.

The wife continued, "Come on, Honey. It's almost time for church and if you don't get up right now we are going to be late."

The exhausted husband started showing some signs of life. "Why don't we just sleep in this morning? I know the good Lord would forgive us for missing church one Sunday. Why don't we just spend some time together and go out to breakfast this morning."

"Come on, Honey. We have to get going right now. It's Sunday and we need to get to church," she persisted.

"Why do we have to go to church all the time anyway?" the husband grunted. "If you can tell me three good reasons why we should go to church, then I'll get up and get ready and we'll go."

"Well," the wife said, "the Bible does say to not forsake the assembling of ourselves together on the first day of the week as is the habit of some."

"That's true," the husband said, "but that's just one reason. I said give me three reasons why we should go to church."

"Well, Honey," the wife continued, "you know every time we gather with other believers, we are encouraged in our faith."

"That's true," the hubby said, "but that's just two reasons. I said you had to give me three."

The wife grew very pensive. She thought for a long moment and then said, "Well, Honey, you are the pastor!"

STRIPES

By His stripes, we were healed.

ISAIAH 53:5

"THERE MUST BE A PURPOSE to all of this," I thought, as I walked into Howard Hall. It was welcoming day at military school. The first soldier I met greeted me with a sinister grin and circled my head with a shaver. I was in shock from losing all my hair so abruptly. The wool from the West Point uniform was scratchy and uncomfortable and the hat they issued me was way too tight on my head. "Dad sent me here . . . so it must be for a purpose."

The weeks and months that followed were filled with formations, marching drills, and white glove inspections. We squared our meals and our shoulders. We cleaned our plates, our rifles, and our rooms, and shouted "Sir, yes, Sir" at the top of our lungs. The cadets of B Company shared many hard earned lessons. We learned discipline, duty, and honor, and to salute when the Stars and Stripes were raised. Never had I felt so alone . . . never had I been so very far from home.

It was just before the commencement exercises when I got my sergeant's stripes. My Dad was so proud. He had been a captain in World War II. I think my father loved me most on the day I got my stripes.

As I reminisce about my time at General Douglas MacArthur Military Academy, I'm reminded of my father's favorite verse: "For God so loved the world that he gave his one and only Son, . . ." (John 3:16). I wonder if Jesus was in shock when He lost His beard so abruptly, or if the soldiers met Him with a sinister grin. How hard it must have been for Him to wear His purple robe . . . how sharp His crown of thorns must have been, so tightly fitted on His head.

"For the joy set before him he endured the cross, . . ." (Hebrews 12:2b) the writer of Hebrews says. Yet nothing is said of how lonely He must have felt, so very far from home. Could it be the Father loved Him most on the day He got His stripes?

Oh, Christian, think it not a small thing, this duty He saw through. The whip, the cross, the empty tomb were given for you and me. He loves us in the valley. . . He loves us on mountain heights.

I think the Father loves us most on days we get our stripes!

A Tither's Confidence

God has not given us a spirit of fear.

II Timothy 1:7

TWO MEN CRASHED IN THEIR private plane on a South Pacific island. Both survived. One of the men brushed himself off and then proceeded to run all over the island to see if they had any chance of survival. When he returned, he rushed up to the other man and screamed, "This island is uninhabited, there is no food, there is no water. We are going to die!"

The other man leaned back against the fuselage of the wrecked plane, folded his arms, and responded, "No, we're not going to die. I make more than $100,000 a week."

The first man grabbed his friend and shook him. "Listen, we are on an uninhabited island. There is no food or water. We are going to die!"

The other man, still unruffled, again responded, "No, we're not going to die. I make over $100,000 a week."

Mystified, the first man, taken aback with such an answer again repeated, "For the last time, I'm telling you we are doomed. There is no one else on the island. There is no food. There is no water. We are, I repeat, we are going to die."

Still unfazed, the first man looked the other in the eyes and said, "Don't make me say this again. We are not going to die. I make more than $100,000 a week, and I tithe ten percent. . . . My pastor will find us!"

The Man from Galilee

Jesus returned to Galilee in the power of the Spirit.
LUKE 4:14

There was a man from Galilee
Who fed the poor and calmed the sea.
He healed the sick, and raised the dead:
He's a blasphemer, the wise men said.

From His mother's holy womb,
Yes, even after the empty tomb
Joseph wondered and the apostles too:
Lord Jesus Christ, is it really you?

Thirty-three years went rolling by
Before our Lord Jesus was told to die.
Father, oh Father, please take this death bed.
But not my will, Father—your will instead.

It was in that garden,
Where He sweated and prayed,
The Lord Jesus Christ
Was soon betrayed.

They whipped Him and beat Him
Yes, they killed Him, too.
Did you know that He died
For me and for you?

There was a man from Galilee
Who fed the poor and calmed the sea
And when it all is said and done
You too will know that He's the one.

I hear the gates
To hell are wide
And I want to see you
On the other side.

Oh, listen, please listen,
Is that a trumpet I hear?
Oh listen, please listen,
Judgment day is so near!

So listen and read,
Be humbled and pray
For it is His promise
You too will soon say:

"Praise Jesus of Nazareth;
Thank you, dear Lord."
Yes, Jesus of Nazareth:
Jesus is Lord!

They're Beautiful

To the pure, all things are pure.

TITUS 1:15

NEW JERSEY IS KNOWN AS the Garden State. That's where I was born. That's where I grew up. It wasn't unusual for the homes in our neighborhood to have beautiful gardens all around them. Our home was unusual in many ways. However, in this one regard, our home was not different from most. Our front yard was the home of three gardens.

To teach us responsibility and that work was more than just a four-letter word, my dad assigned each of those gardens to the care of my two sisters and me. Each of us had our own garden. For a five-year old boy, that was a pretty big deal! My eldest sister, Tica, cared for the largest garden. Like Tica, it was always beautiful and well groomed. Roxie's garden was smaller than Tica's, but larger than mine. Perhaps fitting for the middle child, Roxie's seemed to be the most colorful. I was the baby in the family. My garden was a long row of tulips that ran along side of the house. Sometimes my friend K.J. and I would catch a mess of fish down at Deefy Leaves and bury them in the garden as fertilizer. Many Saturdays, while we were raking the yard or tending the garden, we would watch our friends riding by on their bicycles. As a kid, I resented my dad making us work in the yard. As a man, I'm so thankful he did. He gave each of us his work ethic.

One spring morning, I found myself wondering around the house looking for something to do. I noticed that my tulip garden was in full bloom. I thought to myself, "I bet Mommy would like these flowers." So I took a pair of scissors and cut every one of those tulips, right under the flower, destroying the entire garden. I gathered up the pile of tulip tops in the makeshift pouch I had created with my T-shirt and brought them in the house. "Mommy, I brought you a present," I shouted, as I walked into the house. In a glimpse, my mom surmised exactly what had just taken place. She paused a moment and then exclaimed, "They're beautiful!" She then filled a large crystal bowl with water and lovingly placed the floating tulip-tops on the dining room table. It wasn't until many years later that I realized what a special gift I had been given. Today I understand what James, the brother of Jesus, meant when he said "Mercy triumphs over judgment" (James 2:13b).

Forty-five years later, Dad is pushing ninety. In His own way he's still working hard. Now he spends his days at Greynold Park Nursing Home in North Miami. From time to time he gets out behind the nursing home and checks up on the gardens there. Mom, well, she went to help Jesus "prepare a place for us." When we get there, I won't be a bit surprised if my sisters and I don't find tulip-tops floating in the Crystal Sea. Thanks, Mom.

How God Feels About the Lost

by Jean Brissey

I WAS RAISED IN A religion that struck fear in my heart. I was taught that by saying religious, repetitive prayers and if I was "good," then one day I might escape the flames of hell. All through my childhood, I found it difficult to sleep because of all the fear that was put into my mind. I had no assurance, no hope that God truly loved me and that I would be with Him one day in heaven when I died. Sadly, there was no one available to me in my church, my family, or my friends to lead me to Christ: to the truth and to His peace. I would have gladly received Him as a child. I had a hungry and open heart and wanted desperately to feel His love. I often meet others with a similar background, and I find they have no real assurance of heaven. Some seem satisfied with their hopes of heaven, but others I know live in fear. My heart breaks for them, because I know what religion without a relationship with God can do to one's soul.

The Holy Spirit woke me up one night and had me feel the condition of so many of His people. I literally felt what they feel. It was so very real to me, because the way they felt was the way I lived my childhood—in fear of not really knowing Him—in fear of hell. Jesus said we would go to proclaim truth, salvation, and freedom to His people. What I heard was very dramatic and life changing. I've burned before with the desire to get to the people who need us, who are crying out to God, but now I am desperate to get to them. The Lord said to me "I want you to feel what I feel for the lost." I am starting to feel more and more the heart and emotions of our God. He is compassionate, full of mercy and grace, desperate to use His faithful ones to be His hands and feet to the lost, hurting, and desperate people of the world. The time is short and He is positioning His people to line up, draw close to Him, hear His voice, and go where He calls them to go and do what He calls them to do.

The Lord spoke to me eight years ago that when the greater level of glory and anointing is released upon the earth, so will more demons of hell come and try to destroy God's people. He said "you will see men fall to the left and the right, but your house will stand strong." We have all seen ministers fall, not able to sustain the onslaught and attack of the enemy. Our house was also mightily shaken. Over the years we have gone through situations where we wanted to give up and die. Yet, God has sustained us: He made us stronger and brought us through.

The enemy has used television, movies, and the internet to grip his people into the seduction of pornography, lust, violence, murder, and witchcraft. If I'm speaking to you right now, make steps to clean your home and make it holy. To purify our homes we can block out those things that can cause spirits of deception and perversion to infiltrate our families. We have a choice to make our home a safe haven where the Holy Spirit and His angels are happy to dwell. Matthew 5:27–29 says, "You have heard that it was said, 'You shall not commit adultery.' But I tell you that anyone who looks at a woman lustfully has already committed adultery with her in his heart. If your right eye causes you to stumble, gouge it out and throw it away . . ." I say if your computer causes you to sin, rip it out of the wall and throw it out the window.

If your television causes you to sin, take a sledge hammer and smash in the screen, jump on it three times, then take it to the dumpster. My point is this: purify your homes and hearts! And let God use you as a vessel of honor in these last days.

The enemy has always tried to seduce children in witchcraft, very subtly in cartoons and movies. But now witchcraft is out in the open, with movies such as *Harry Potter*. After that movie, thousands searched the internet for witchcraft sites to learn more about how they also could have magical powers. The devil is no gentleman. He's after your marriage, family, finances, and ministry. What's the answer to this dark and glorious day of the Lord? To love, receive, and accept the precious Holy Spirit within and all that He longs to do through you and his church. Draw near to Him and love Him. God wants to position you. There is an acceleration going on right now in the spirit realm, and He is calling you to be a lover of what He loves: the lost.

If you have fallen under the pressure, assault, and attack of the enemy and his henchmen, pick yourself up, share your sins with a trusted leader or servant of God, forgive yourself, receive Christ's forgiveness, and press into the call He has placed on your life. My husband had a vision years ago that powerfully affected his life, and I will let him share it:

Jim:

In 1981, I was in the Spirit in prayer, and the Lord spoke to me through a picture that was played in my mind like a video. It was a moving picture of Jesus on the cross. He was being crucified, but was still on the cross in agony. The picture started from a far distance, but slowly zoomed in. As the picture drew closer to Jesus on the cross, I saw a man standing in front of the cross, spitting on Jesus. As the picture drew closer, coming in from behind the man's right shoulder, . . . I suddenly saw that man was me! "No, Lord!" I cried in my spirit, "I would never spit on you or your cross!" The Lord spoke to me words that have continued to echo in my heart until this very moment: "Every time you don't forgive yourself, that is exactly what you are doing!" That was the day I accepted forgiveness from myself!

As I was worshipping God today while lying on my bed, He started to shake me from my head to my toes. He said He wanted to use me to shake His people . . . shake, shake, shake . . . His people right into their calling—right into their destiny. This is it! Now's the time! Today is the day to take your position in the army of God! The requirement for your enlistment (I'm so glad you asked) is this: to live a holy righteous life, crushed and humbled before God and His people, and to count yourself nothing, so that He can be everything. Philippians 2:5–9 says, "In your relationships with one another, have the same mindset as Christ Jesus: Who, being in very nature God, did not consider equality with God something to be used to his own advantage; rather, he made himself nothing by taking the very nature of a servant, being made in human likeness. And being found in appearance as a man, he humbled himself by becoming obedient to death—even death on a cross! Therefore God exalted him to the highest place and gave him the name that is above every name, . . ."

I spent so many years as a Christian filled with pride and a controlling spirit. Because I refused to submit myself to anyone, I fell dramatically on my face time and again. I was totally deceived in these areas. I was completely blinded and I hurt a lot of people, especially my husband. It's been a slow change for me; but at this time in my life I desperately want to trust, submit, and surrender. So many of us control because we have been so wounded and we feel we need to protect ourselves. Fear is the backbone of control. It's time to let go and trust God fully with our lives. We have all been abused and broken, but God is the great physician and He can heal you everywhere you hurt. He wants to heal you! But many of us walk around poisoned by resentment and bitterness. Let go and let God restore you; He will and He can. BELIEVE HIM! Lay your lives down at the cross of Christ and allow Him to crush you, so that you might rise up as a mighty warrior, able to heal the broken hearts of the masses who are coming in very, very soon. GET READY—GET READY—God is sounding the trumpet: can you feel it? Can you feel the change in the spiritual realm? There will be hard times to come upon this earth, and thousands will be coming to Christ. We need the body of Christ to be aware, awake, and ready. You have been privileged to live in these last days.

My precious husband has been preaching this year "change, declare, and prepare." He said he feels the Lord might never release him from this message. Change is our first line of business. I'm horrified at the body of Christ given over to the flesh, and flaky and fruity spirituality. Wake up, crucify the flesh, and take your rightful place in the body as one of the King's kids, armed for battle. Every day we all have choices to make—what to wear, what to eat, where to go, what to say, what to watch—our natural fleshly sinful self would love to eat Big Macs, fries, and shakes as opposed to a fresh salad, vegetables, grilled chicken, and water. We love to look at the negative and tear down our brother and sister instead of encouraging and building them up. We love to watch movies with lots of sex, violence, murder, and horror movies (evil personified), as opposed to wholesome, clean, Christian movies.

What's the answer to this stinking flesh? A close, committed, dedicated, disciplined, fire-filled, desperate hunger and thirst for God in our lives. We have no ability in ourselves to change. Only the work of the Holy Spirit within can do the much-needed job.

You who are reading this book, He is after you. He is in heavy pursuit of you to grab hold of your life. He wants to purify you for the awesome privilege of going after the lost (the end-time harvest). WAKE UP; WAKE UP! Some of you received words years and years ago about your calling: this is it, this is the time! He is preparing, purifying, and will be sending His army out now to the outer parts of the earth. There are places right now that have never heard the gospel. He will speak to His people and specifically lead them to places no man can ever find.

Supernatural happenings will be the norm. God's people will be transported from place to place, where miracles, healings, deliverance, and salvation will occur. How do we line up with God to be used in this glorious way? Make an appointment with God every day, and spend time in His Spirit. Listen for His voice and instruction and ask the Holy Spirit to help you make choices for righteousness each day. Read His word, knowing that His word is alive, and by faith let His word wash you and transform your mind and spirit. Make choices to feed your spirit man more than you feed your fleshly man. Build up your spirit by praying in the spirit, which will edify your spirit. Also, know that the Holy Spirit says the most perfect prayers through you (Romans 8:26). Be filled with His word, and have a close relationship with the Holy Spirit throughout the day. What's so exciting about living a close love walk with God? There is so much victory, love, peace, and joy in your life. A close relationship with God is the adventure of a lifetime. He is fun, He is exciting, and He is new every day. What a faithful, fun, and glorious friend He is!

My daughter and I have recently decided to have an appointment with God at 5:00 a.m. every day. We make appointments for the doctor, for lunch dates, for haircuts, etc., so why not meet and have intimacy with the greatest friend in the world? For those who know me, getting up at 4:45 a.m. is an act of God, because sleeping is something I love to do. I have always had low energy, even as a child. It is only God who has made me feel more alive and more energetic to accomplish this sacrifice. My husband and others are starting to join us at our church at 5:00 a.m. Our focus is on renewal. God called us to this region for the purpose of renewal. We have found religion, witchcraft, and cold love to be the norm here; it has been discouraging and heartbreaking. But God speaks to us every morning concerning the effectiveness of our prayers for our city. All He wants is for His children to come to Him, love Him, sit on His lap, and wait on Him—to rest in His beautiful, peaceful presence so He can love us, comfort us, instruct us, and change us. Oh, I'm sorry; *change* is a dirty word; people hate change. But change must come before destiny is fulfilled. 1 Peter

5:6–9 says, "Humble yourselves, therefore, under God's mighty hand, that he may lift you up in due time. Cast all your anxiety on him because he cares for you. Be alert and of sober mind. Your enemy the devil prowls around like a roaring lion looking for someone to devour. Resist him, standing firm in the faith, because you know that the family of believers throughout the world is undergoing the same kind of sufferings."

Years ago we went to a meeting in Tampa, FL, where we saw a video from Africa of over one million souls coming to Christ at one time. My husband and I stood there in the sanctuary and wept. God was convicting us and stirring us out of our complacency for the souls all around us. At that moment we realized that we had put our personal soul-winning on the shelf for so many years. Even though in all of our meetings in prisons, nursing homes, and churches, we always give the people opportunities to receive the Lord, we no longer witnessed to people in our everyday life.

Another astonishing revelation came when we found out that the people in our church (even those who were Christians for twenty years) did not even know how to win a soul to Christ! We have always allowed our people to preach, but now we are teaching them how to give altar calls. On Wednesday nights we are having classes on how to lead a person to Christ, what to say, and how to pray. At the end of this section I will give you some words, scripture, and prayers to say to those the Lord leads you to. You first want to have a good prayer life yourself. Then you just ask the Holy Spirit to lead you to those who need to hear about our wonderful Lord. Be real; be yourself! Use genuine, normal words!

Many years ago, when my husband and I were visiting my mother-in-law in the hospital, there was a woman in the next bed who kept on talking to us, trying to get out attention. We wanted to visit my mother-in-law and found this other woman's talking very annoying. As we were trying to ignore her, the Spirit got through my stubborn mind and said, "Go to her!" She was a ninety-year-old Jewish woman. She had died nine times, and she didn't understand why she was still alive. I said, "You are still alive because the Lord Jesus wants to come into your life." She said, "I have wanted to do that all of my life." She said she had asked the hospital to send a minister and he had been there yesterday. So I asked her if the minister showed her the way to Christ and prayed for her? She said "No, he just said a silent prayer for me." "Well, would you like to receive Jesus as your Lord and Savior right now?" I replied. "Yes," she said, and we prayed together. Afterward she said she felt a heavy weight lift right off her chest. Praise God! What a privilege it was to lead this Jewish woman to Christ that day.

When we read the book of Acts, we can see the kind of suffering and persecution the apostles went through to lead souls to Christ. The more persecution, the more fire-fueled they were to spread the gospel of Jesus Christ. Here we are fat, sassy, lazy, sleeping, and free American Christians who can't remember the last person we led to Christ. We are not persecuted, chained, flogged, or sent to jail. But our passion for souls is almost extinct. To the sleeping cold church of America, the Lord says "WAKE UP! HELLO, IT'S TIME—YES YOU—I'M TALKING TO YOU—TURN OFF THE TV, PUT THOSE CHIPS DOWN, GET UP—GET READY!" Look at the saints in China. They have to hide to go to church. Some only have one page of the Bible that they hang on to for dear life. They are tortured and killed for Christ everyday! HELLO; WAKE UP. Acts 11:19–21 says, "Now those who had been scattered by the persecution that broke out when Stephen was killed traveled as far as Phoenicia, Cyprus and Antioch, spreading the word only among Jews. Some of them, however, men from Cyprus and Cyrene, went to Antioch and began to speak to Greeks also, telling them the good news about the Lord Jesus. The Lord's hand was with them, and a great number of people believed and turned to the Lord."

The churches in the disciples' day met at church to worship, and then blessed and sent out servants to preach the gospel all over the region. We as pastors need to train, equip, and send our people out to win the lost. God wants to use the whole body in these end times. We need to leave the four walls of our church to affect our community and the world. If you're a pastor, I would encourage you to put more emphasis on outreaches and missions. If we don't go, who will? Let our prayer be, "Here am I Lord, send me!" If you truly don't feel led to go (as long as you don't have lead poisoning) say, "Lord, here am I, I will pay for someone else to go"—and you will reap the same rewards. God needs obedient, generous people as much as He needs willing servants to travel to the ends of the earth. You can't take your money with you when you go; I've never seen a hearse pulling a U-Haul.

It costs money to go to the ends of the earth. We have been so blessed to lead several mission teams to Honduras. It costs $1,800 for each person. God uses obedient Christians like you and me to give and make it happen. I pray that God will begin to deal with those wealthy people, fearfully hanging onto their money. I pray that they will surrender it for the work of the Lord. There is so much work to be done, so many places to go before the end will come. We need to rise up as the body of Christ and work together to advance the gospel.

I pray that He is speaking to you today. The word says, ". . . he who wins souls is wise" (Proverbs 11:30b NKJV). My husband and I feel that the greatest aspect of our ministry is when we are privileged by the Lord to see souls won. We feel there is no greater joy in all the world. You know, the only thing you can take with you when you die is souls.

Statistics show that forty percent of people going to liturgical churches have never been born again. It is up to us to make sure that our circle of family, friends, and acquaintances know the truth and come to a living faith in Jesus Christ. Our cousin Henry was a Lutheran pastor for fifteen years, until one day he met Jesus personally and was born again. Years ago I was led to talk to a sixteen-year-old girl about the Lord. I lead her in the sinner's prayer; the next day she died in a tragic car accident. Always be ready and obedient to speak to those whom God puts on your heart.

When I was twenty-seven years old, my husband and I received our life's call and marching orders from the Lord. As we were reading Isaiah 61, the words "illuminated" off the page and we were filled with the Spirit of God. The experience is as fresh to me today as it was then. The Word says, "The Spirit of the Sovereign Lord is on me, because the Lord has anointed me to proclaim good news to the poor. He has sent me to bind up the brokenhearted, to proclaim freedom for the captives and release from darkness for the prisoners, to proclaim the year of the Lord's favor and the day of vengeance of our God, to comfort all who mourn, and provide for those who grieve in Zion—to bestow on them a crown of beauty instead of ashes, the oil of joy instead of mourning, and a garment of praise instead of a spirit of despair. They will be called oaks of righteousness, a planting of the Lord for the display of his splendor" (Isaiah 61:1-3).

For some of you reading this right now, you are saying, "Yes, Lord, this is my destiny, my call to bring light to the dark places, hope to the hopeless, and joy instead of sadness to the hurting world around me."

On an extremely cold night in December, 1995, my former dance leader brought a team of Christians to go to the streets of Ybor City in Tampa to share the gospel. It was Christmas time and we had the three kings, Mary and Joseph, and of course angels who did an interpretive dance with a short gospel message to follow. We were quite the sight walking down the streets of party town all dressed up in our costumes.

The funny part is, no one really looked at us or laughed at us. Well, one man came out of a bar and laughed, but that was it. Debbie and I were angels. Unlike real angels, we were freezing! As we went through our routine, all we had for our audience was one homeless, alcoholic man. No one else was interested, but this one man was mesmerized. We told him we would be back the next night. He came early and helped us carry our equipment to a new street. We went through our routine with my husband preaching a short message. Again our only audience was this homeless man. His heart was melting as he saw the gospel re-enacted and heard the preaching of the word.

My husband asked him if he would like to ask Jesus in his heart. With tears in his eyes he received Jesus and found new life. All the practice, all the work, standing in the freezing cold, three nights, just for this one half-Jewish, alcoholic man. YES, YES, YES! If you were the only person in the world, He still would have died for you. Mickey Z. was his name. We brought him that night to a church that had a program for alcoholics. He became the pastor's assistant and stayed sober. Twenty years later, Mickey continues to serve in our church. He is sober and joyful. He has stumbled a couple of times, but the Lord has restored him. He shares his testimony at our outreaches.

In order to find God's chosen people, we need to leave the comfy pews and go out into the world. Instead of praying for the lost, we need to go to the lost. We were at a church a few years ago when the pastor said "Everyone extend your hands to the door and pray for the souls." The visiting guest speaker got up and said "I didn't see anyone walk through those doors, did you?" We need to get out of the four walls of the church.

Last year the Lord spoke a word to me; He said, "I am going to resurrect the dead in Christ." I knew

How God Feels About the Lost 133

instantly what He meant. He was referring to those who once served the Lord, but left the church because of the gross sins of the leadership of the church, those who put their trust in man only to be betrayed, and those who have been crushed and lost for years. In this region God has called us to, the churches have been ravaged with sin. Hundreds of disillusioned people don't want anything to do with God or church again. God is going after his hurting and lost children, and He wants to use all of us to help bring healing to them and bring them back under the umbrella of protection in the church. God's heart, His emotions, are compelling his people to go—to feel what He feels for the lost of this world. Please listen to His voice and heed His call. He wants to use you and me as His hands and feet. Will you pray about going?

We are seeing come into our church, one by one, those whom God is bringing back into His fold. A woman who has been out of church has just come back to our church. She was hurt by a church and wanted nothing to do with church any longer. She is now blossoming like a flower. A man who was hurt by the church due to extreme legalism, after ten years now comes to our church and cries through the whole service. God is bringing home His precious babies that He loves. If you are one of the disillusioned or hurting, know that God loves you with an everlasting love. He will never leave you, never forget you, and never stop loving you. Man will sin and fail you, but God is perfect, loving, and forgiving. He holds His hands out to you and patiently waits for your return. Just like the prodigal son, whose father was overjoyed with emotion to welcome his sinful son back into his house, our God extends his arms to you, just as a loving daddy would do. Isaiah says, "He has sent me to bind up the brokenhearted, to proclaim freedom for the captives and release from darkness for the prisoners, . . ." (Isaiah 61:1b).

Speaking of the prisoners, our ministry has been going into the prisons for over twenty years. We have been blessed to see more than 4,500 souls come to the Lord. We know we are making a difference, especially when we get letters from prisoners such as Jessie. He starts his letter with a vivid description of the abuse he endured as a child, but then he says, "But Mr. Brissey, when you and your people come I feel something, even if it is only a little something. When you preach, you hold my attention and that girl that dresses up like a clown, every time she speaks and tells about herself she damn near pulls tears from my eyes. The little Spanish women pulls my heart strings. Your wife is funny and makes me laugh. There isn't too much in this world that makes me laugh but she does. Your daughter, how can she be so happy? I've been trying for 32 years and can't be. I want what they have. Why do you people make me feel this way? I won't let you pray for me, or any of that other stuff. But PLEASE keep coming back, 'cuz you bring something with you. I'm not a Christian and I know I'm not saved and don't know what is going on inside of me. All I know is the hate and anger I feel every day. I do want to change though, I just don't know what to do. But PLEASE . . . Just come back because I really enjoy you and your people and what you bring with you, Jessie." Not long before his release from prison, Jessie received Jesus as his Lord and Savior. God's desire is for you and me to bring light into the dark places of the world. If you and I don't go . . . who will?

"Change, declare, and prepare" is God's word for you today. Isaiah 61:7 says, "Instead of your shame you will receive a double portion, and instead of disgrace you will rejoice in your inheritance. And so you will inherit a double portion in your land, and everlasting joy will be yours". Receive His joy and receive your inheritance! Be filled with the Holy Spirit and proclaim the good news of the gospel. Talk to people at the supermarket, malls, restaurants, etc. Keep your spiritual eyes and ears open to the still small voice of the Holy Spirit within you.

Acts 1:7–8 says "It is not for you to know the times or dates the Father has set by his own authority. But you will receive power when the Holy Spirit comes on you; and you will be my witnesses in Jerusalem, and in all Judea and Samaria, and to the ends of the earth". I pray you will be His witness. Start where you are. He will lead you. I pray for you that you will be obedient and listen for your instructions from heaven where you are to go, what you are to do, and what you are to say. I want to give you a general script that you can study as a helpful tool to lead people to Christ. As you pray and the Lord leads you to someone, you can start by saying:

- Did you know that God loves you and has a wonderful plan for your life?

- If they say "Yes," ask "Do you know beyond a shadow of a doubt that if you died tonight you would be with Jesus in heaven?"

- If they say, "Yes, I hope so" or "I think so" or "I know I am going to heaven because I am a good person" say . . .

- "Romans 3:23 says, 'for all have sinned and fall short of the glory of God'".

- 1 John 1:8-9 says, "If we claim to be without sin, we deceive ourselves and the truth is not in us. If we confess our sins, he is faithful and just and will forgive us our sins and purify us from all unrighteousness".

- Say, *"Jesus died on the cross for your sins and my sins. All we need to do is acknowledge the price Jesus paid on the cross, say we are sorry for our sins and ask Jesus to come into our heart. It is a free gift. Would you like to ask the Lord in your heart right now?"*

> ❧ If they say yes, tell them to just repeat this prayer after you. *"Lord, I thank you for dying on the cross for me; please forgive me for having sinned against you. Lord, I ask you to come into my heart and make me a new creation. I will love you and live for you all the days of my life. Amen."*

Be blessed! Serve the Lord with gladness and bring many souls to heaven with you!

About the Authors

JIM AND JEAN BRISSEY ARE Senior Pastors of Higher Ground Ministries in DeLand, Fl. Jim earned his Bachelor of Biblical Studies through Omega Seminary. Jean is a graduate of Spirit Life School of Theology. Jim & Jean have been married for 37 years. They are ordained through Revival Ministries International in Tampa, Fl. Jim & Jean have spearheaded hundreds of outreaches throughout the U.S. and abroad and have witnessed thousands give their heart to Jesus. They have a passion for revival, evangelistic outreach and training outreach ministers.

Higher Ground
School of Ministry

Anointed – Relevant – Affordable – Scripturally Sound

- Committed to providing quality ministry training & credentials to effectively further the Kingdom of God.
- Classes are available online, in person or by way of correspondence.
- Students may start at any time and move forward at their own pace without pressure or obligation.

www.highergroundministries.org

Higher Ground Ministries
820 N. Frankfort Avenue
P.O. Box 1313
DeLand, Florida 32721
higherground_1@msn.com
(386) 738-7077

For more information about
Jim Brissey
&
A Shepherd's Heart
please visit:

Website: www.highergroundministries.org
Email: higherground_1@msn.com
Facebook: www.facebook.com/jimbrissey

For more information about
AMBASSADOR INTERNATIONAL
please visit:

www.ambassador-international.com
@AmbassadorIntl
www.facebook.com/AmbassadorIntl